# Divination Explained

Divination Overview, History, Types, the Art of Divination, Symbolic Thought, Advance Techniques and More!

By Riley Star

**Copyrights and Trademarks**

All rights reserved. No part of this book may be reproduced or transformed in any form or by any means, graphic, electronic, or mechanical, including photocopying, recording, taping, or by any information storage retrieval system, without the written permission of the author.

This publication is Copyright ©2020. Nevada. All products, graphics, publications, software and services mentioned and recommended in this publication are protected by trademarks. In such instance, all trademarks & copyright belong to the respective owners. For information consult www.NRBpublishing.com

**Disclaimer and Legal Notice**

This product is not legal, medical, or accounting advice and should not be interpreted in that manner. You need to do your own due-diligence to determine if the content of this product is right for you. While every attempt has been made to verify the information shared in this publication, neither the author, neither publisher, nor the affiliates assume any responsibility for errors, omissions or contrary interpretation of the subject matter herein. Any perceived slights to any specific person(s) or organization(s) are purely unintentional.

We have no control over the nature, content and availability of the web sites listed in this book. The inclusion of any web site links does not necessarily imply a recommendation or endorse the views expressed within them. We take no responsibility for, and will not be liable for, the websites being temporarily unavailable or being removed from the internet.

The accuracy and completeness of information provided herein and opinions stated herein are not guaranteed or warranted to produce any particular results, and the advice and strategies, contained herein may not be suitable for every individual. Neither the author nor the publisher shall be liable for any loss incurred as a consequence of the use and application, directly or indirectly, of any information presented in this work. This publication is designed to provide information in regard to the subject matter covered. Neither the author nor the publisher assume any responsibility for any errors or omissions, nor do they represent or warrant that the ideas, information, actions, plans, suggestions contained in this book is in all cases accurate. It is the reader's responsibility to find advice before putting anything written in this book into practice. The information in this book is not intended to serve as legal, medical, or accounting advice.

# Foreword

Recent years have seen quite an explosion when it comes to the topic about discovering one's future, dealing with the now, and even practice attracting or working with the so – called "Law of Attraction." There are now many psychic telephone lines that are available 24/7, and most of them have established a certain market segment. Programs like Book of Changes and rune reading have been installed on personal computers while tarot decks or tarot card reading are becoming more popular than ever.

Major psychic fairs now attract thousands of attendees that are eager to see a glimpse of what the future holds for them which is proof that we all are curious to see what tomorrow will bring. The goals for knowing the future varies from one person to another but the desire is as old as human perception of time and consciousness.

Modern technology may have adapted ancient forms of fortune telling but the old ways are still used by many psychics and subjects who want to personally connect to their potential paths in life. This is perhaps one of the greatest values of divination – we are innate diviners.

This book will guide you on how you can use divine techniques and also in understanding ancient wisdom and knowledge that you can use to improve your lives.

# Table of Contents

Introduction ........................................................................... 1

Chapter One: Overview of Divination ................................. 5

    How Divination Works ................................................... 8

    The Major Types of Divination ...................................... 9

    The Divinatory Response ............................................. 10

    Divination Isn't Psychic Awareness ............................ 12

    The Past is Important ................................................... 13

Chapter Two: Divination during Ancient Times ............. 17

    Divination in Babylon .................................................. 18

    Divination in Rome ...................................................... 20

    Divination in Ancient Germany ................................. 21

    Divination in Tibet ....................................................... 22

Chapter Three: The Art of Divination ............................... 25

    The Appropriate Attitude ............................................ 26

    The Question ................................................................. 28

    Repetition of Divination .............................................. 31

    Preparing Prior to Divination ..................................... 31

Appropriate Times for Divination ................................................ 33

Interpreting Symbolic Responses .............................................. 34

A Lack of Response ...................................................................... 34

Chapter Four: Symbolic Thought ................................................... 37

How You Can Develop Symbolic Thought ............................... 45

Chapter Five: The Nature of Time in Divination ......................... 47

Chapter Six: Altering Your Future .................................................. 53

Karma .............................................................................................. 55

Action and Thought to Prevent Negative Future Events ...... 57

Chapter Seven: Advance Technique Part I .................................... 61

The Book of Changes in Divination ........................................... 62

The Yin and Yang .......................................................................... 63

The Theory of Ideas ...................................................................... 65

The Judgments .............................................................................. 67

How to Use the Book of Changes ............................................... 69

Chapter Eight: Advance Techniques Part II .................................. 75

Chiromancy in Divination .......................................................... 76

Physical Factors ............................................................................. 79

Active vs. Passive Zones ........................................................ 81

Texture of Palm ...................................................................... 84

Consistency ............................................................................. 88

Hand Flexibility ..................................................................... 92

The Mounts ............................................................................. 93

Tarot in Divination ................................................................ 98

Chapter Ten: Conclusion ..................................................... 129

Index ...................................................................................... 133

PHOTO REFERENCES ......................................................... 137

REFERENCES ........................................................................ 139

# Introduction

In our relatively short history, we have always been riddled with anxieties, hopes and questions as to what tomorrow will be like for us. Though in many ways plants and even animals are better predictors of certain phenomenon such as weather forecasts, our species overtime have developed various techniques that are designed to go through the veil that divides tomorrow from today.

One of the primary uses of divination today is to make difficult choices, to examine the present, and gain a clear sense of the past. This art has been referred to by many

# Introduction

names; some call it "fortune - telling" or "psychic prediction" but these are somewhat derogatory terms. Most experts refer to ancient art as simply "divination," and they define themselves as "diviners."

This book is a complete guide to the art of determining your past, present and future. We don't need to have psychic abilities per se to discover what the past, present and future is telling us, and that's a good thing because it only means that anyone can practice this ancient art and be able to receive information from a higher source. This book will show you various methods to do that.

The first part consists of an overview of the topic including the importance of divination during the time of our ancestors. It also included various techniques of symbolic thought, the nature of an illusion we refer to as time and also a workable plan to alter an unwanted future.

On the next few chapters of the book, you will learn about the detailed descriptions of an array of divinatory techniques. Each of these techniques and are grouped along with the tools you can use to perform them; many of them

## Introduction

uses forces that can be found in nature such as fire, water, bird movements, smoke, douds and the likes.

*Divination Explained* is a practical guide book to a very practical ancient art. This information is presented to the reader with the intention of providing ways for seeing possible outcomes, offering assistance whenever one is dealing with a hard decision and answer other question that may concern the past, present and future.

Just like any other self – help book or divination books, there is no guarantee of success in any of the techniques that will be presented here but it will be unlikely that the ancient art will survive for over 5 millennia if it wasn't effective would it? So I urge you to just keep an open mind and apply the techniques here and see what works and what doesn't. Give it time to unfold and trust the process.

Divination isn't a step backward into the times that humans were largely ruled by misunderstanding and superstition but instead it is more of the true understanding of the universal forces at work in our lives. The forces that create our lives need careful thoughts as well as

# Introduction

reconsideration especially when it comes to some interesting concepts that we hold dear. There is no such thing as fate or destiny. No higher force determines how our life will go because it is almost totally in our hands. There could be a path set for us by the universe but it is not absolute, and it can change if we choose to and if we know how to collaborate with such forces.

Divination can be a powerful tool that provides otherwise unknowable information but most importantly it can be a great ally in reshaping our lives and align it with our dreams and hopes. Divination is all about searching the past, examining the present and looking into the future; only then will you be prepared to become part of a great adventure we call "life."

# Chapter One: Overview of Divination

Divination is the art of determining the unknown through the observation and manipulation of tools recognized by the users as possessing the ability to provide insights. The ancient art of divination has never really become unpopular. Even in today's materialistic and high – tech world, we perform age – old rituals and rites to discover what the future holds for us. In its many forms, this ancient art is as much part of our lives today as it is during the time of our ancestors.

## Chapter One: Overview of Divination

The practice of foretelling the future by using techniques pre – dates history which is why there wasn't any record of the first ever culture who acted upon its desire to see a glimpse of tomorrow. Perhaps the earliest forms consisted of using nature such as looking into the sea, watching smoke as it arises from a fire and observing the movements or shapes of clouds. During these times, all phenomena were invested with spiritual energies and it makes sense for our ancestors to rely on nature to predict the future.

In the past, various cultures link the art of divination to religion. The god/ goddesses were believed to be willing to provide the people some form of clues or hints, and one can decipher it by using techniques and specific tools which the deities manipulated to provide the diviner a specific response. The earliest practitioners of the craft though that divination revealed the will of the deities, and that the future was unchangeable. However, after many centuries of practice, diviners eventually realized that such concept can easily be challenged and may not be absolute.

## Chapter One: Overview of Divination

Why some events revealed never did actually happen? Weren't the gods in total control of the lives of all human and the whole universe? Some cultures answered these questions through altering their definition and perception of divination. Rather than revealing an absolute and fated future, divination is now defined as somewhat of a guide to the possible things that may happen. They realized that the future can somehow be altered by action. Thus, divination only provides us a potential view of the future – not of fate. Negative occurrences or symbols are not considered as fate but only useful warnings which means that everything can still change and there is no guarantee.

Today, divination is now considered as a branch of magic. This is not accurate because the two practices are different from one another. Divination attempts to discover what the past, present and future is trying to tell us while magic is more of an active process wherein the future is thought to be changed. Though both practices can be used together, they are still not related and the same. Those who claim that they are clearly have no understanding of both practices.

## Chapter One: Overview of Divination

*How Divination Works*

There are many theories attempting to explain the process at work during divination, but it's not always applicable to all forms. Generally speaking though, it is believed that all our thoughts and action produce non – physical waves of energy that extend into the future and that is shaped into a certain extent. The energy of thoughts and actions produce a map of what tomorrow could bring based on our present direction and speed but there are many destinations that lie on its surface and we always have a choice to change course at any given time.

Divinatory techniques examine such energy waves which usually people are not aware of, and by taking these energies into account, paint a picture of tomorrow should things continue on its present course. The techniques reveal information in various ways. Some of them include the use of sand and also pendulum which seems to rely on the subconscious mind wherein we become aware of such streams in order to produce the response we seek. Other techniques are usually free of our conscious/ subconscious control and only rely on other forces to manipulate tools and

for it to produce a prediction. In these forms, which are usually the most reliable, the tools presented will do the work for us if we allow them.

## The Major Types of Divination

Through studying hundreds of techniques used in different cultures throughout history, diviners have divided the art into two forms: natural and operational.

### **Operational Divination**

It consists of manipulation of tools (ex: oil in water, smoke, dice, stones, eggs, knives, paper etc.) in order to determine the future. These tools are specifically used in such a way that it will express its purpose. These also later represent other divinatory technique.

### **Natural Divination**

It consists of the observation of events or phenomena in the natural world. A specific time and place is usually set aside for it to express a response. For instance, omens are derived from various natural phenomena in the physical world and it is believed to reveal the future. The casual observation of omens that can unexpectedly happen at any time is not true divination. Omens should be preceded by a request for information from the diviner for it to be classified as divination – provoked omens. Many omens are created by the world around us such as the behavior of animals, the stars and clouds, the activity of the wind, appearance of birds, sudden lightning appearance and meteors to name a few.

## The Divinatory Response

Messages received during the process of divination are called "responses." Responses usually take one of three forms. The nature of the technique usually determines the form of the message.

### **Binary Responses**

The techniques that create binary responses are usually receive the clearest answer and easiest to perform.

Questions should be asked that only answers Yes or No – which is why it's binary. Sometimes it can also be answered as "maybe" or "no answer."

## **Symbolic Responses**

The second kind is through the creation of symbols and/or images. The divinatory tools that one uses (such as clouds, water with oil, crystal balls, fire etc.) produce symbols that can be interpreted to answer the question presented by the diviner. Forms that produce such responses are not limited to answering specific question which is why it can be use to effectively determine the general outcome of the future. The symbols that is produce as a response can be interpreted to provide an outlook of the future like "a prosperous year" or "there will be losses" and so on.

Symbolic responses usually rely both on the powers of the diviner's observation and also his/her ability to decipher the inner meanings of the symbols. In general, the symbols that the diviner are familiar with will appear which would enhance his/her ability to have a successful interpretation.

## Chapter One: Overview of Divination

The value of techniques that the binary response produces is obvious which is why no interpretation is needed. Both of the forms however can produce satisfactory result if they are properly used with attitude.

## **Symbolic Thought**

The last type of divination produces what we can call as a selective response. This is when a number of likely future events are written on pieces of stone, paper or leaves and also on other tools. These are then manipulated in order to provide the most likely prediction.

## *Divination Isn't Psychic Awareness*

Many of the processes at work during divination can be understood but there is a fact you need to know – true divination doesn't really need the diviner to have psychic abilities. This is great because it means that anyone – psychic or not – can tap into the universal knowledge that could be unknown to the conscious mind. You can successfully practice divination even if you don't have an innate psychic ability (although I believe all humans have, it's just a matter of practicing it).

It can certainly be true that our psychic minds could be at work during some divination techniques – wherein they examine the energy waves we set out into the future and relate to them to our conscious mind. No such awareness can be at work when one is using selective or binary responses yet all three of them can produce answers that are insightful. Some diviners believe that higher forces manipulate the tools and place symbols for us to see and interpret. The ancient view may or may not be accepted depending on the spiritual beliefs of the diviners.

## The Past is Important

In order to discover what the future holds, we may need to look at the past. This is based on the assumption that we know everything about our pasts since we have lived them. But why do many divinatory techniques focus on the past and future? For instance, tarot spreads include a card that symbolizes the past and future. Magic mirrors and other types of divination tools are also used to illuminate the past.

## Chapter One: Overview of Divination

The answer is simple; every day is how we are building our futures. Every decision that we choose today will affect our lives tomorrow. And usually when we are in a difficult situation, we often ask "Why?" The answer usually lies in the past.

Most of us can remember our pasts but we may not be able to consciously connect the past and present. We are usually incapable of seeing that we reap the fruits of our choices. For instance, if later, you decided to sit in the middle of the road until a car hits you, you will feel the effects of your past decision. If we make unwise choices, we will suffer consequences. If we allow people, society or the world to steer us away from our dreams and goals, we will eventually find ourselves unfulfilled or unhappy. These are just few examples but the thing is that many people are just unable to link their past action to the present life.

The past also affects the future because the energy of the past doesn't only follow us; it races us into the future and continuously molds our lives. This is why becoming aware of the past doesn't just answer the question with regard to our present lives; it can also provide clues of the

## Chapter One: Overview of Divination

future. Therefore, studying the past is an important part of divination.

Divination remains a mysterious art. Education and scientific pursuits mostly stripped us away of the mystery of our lives. Though the purpose of this art is to clarify the future, the manner in which to achieve it is quite evocative and romantic. This is probably why it didn't lose its popularity for 5,000 years.

# Chapter One: Overview of Divination

# Chapter Two: Divination during Ancient Times

Almost every culture has practice some form of divination. This ancient art was not limited to just a few countries – it was actually a worldwide phenomenon. The art of divination is very common in India, Southeast Asia, Africa, the Americas, Australia, China, Japan, Middle East and throughout Europe – virtually it is present in all continents.

## Chapter Two: Divination during Ancient Times

Divination wasn't common in Egypt which is quite surprising as it turns out there are only a few records of divination that existed in Egypt. The greatest number of records was found around the late period of Egyptian history, and most divination techniques of Egyptian were all mixed with Roman, Babylonian and Greek practices. Perhaps the early Egyptians kept such information which is why there is no record of it on temple walls or hieroglyphics. In this chapter, we will give you an idea of how divination was practice among Romans, Babylonians, ancient Germans and Tibetans.

**Divination in Babylon**

As mentioned earlier, divination was used as a method of discovering or knowing the will of the gods/ goddesses/ deities. During the time of the Babylonians, diviners were often needed especially when a national disaster strike or some unwanted incident happened among them. Diviners asked the deities through different rites as to why unfortunate events had occurred. The ancient art was also relied upon often to predict future troubles which is

## Chapter Two: Divination during Ancient Times

why the diviners or their subjects make offerings or do some sort of rituals to protect them or circumvent the foreseen catastrophe.

If, however, the future appears positive, the subject or diviner would pray to the deities as a sign of gratitude and they would also offer appropriate things on the altar. There are lots of techniques that Babylonians used but unfortunately most of these have been lost. The only information that remained came from Akkadian clay tablets that recorded such rituals during the Old Babylonian period. Similar divination techniques were used in Sumer which is a civilization that preceded Babylon.

Some divination practices were reserved for royalties while others are done for those who are in upper class. There were also divination rituals done for the poor since they usually can't afford the necessary sacrifices. Divinatory tools imported from other nations was further developed and used in Babylon. On the other hand, lots of Roman and Greek methods were directly based on the workings of the Babylonians, and as techniques were passed on some of them eventually became complex. Regardless, divination became an exacting art.

## Divination in Rome

There were lots of Roman writers who talked about the subject of divination including Cicero, Aeschylus, Livy and Aeneas but many also made references to the ancient practice. There's actually little reason to doubt the importance of divination in the Roman Empire because back then it was seen as a direct method of communication to the Roman gods and goddesses. Divination was practiced by all social classes and there were many experts that are always being consulted throughout the expansion of Rome's empire. For instance, whenever Rome will go to battle, omens are being consulted. There were also various divination methods but few of which were of local origin. Some methods were created by Etruscans that were eventually passed on to Babylonians, Greeks and also Romans.

## Chapter Two: Divination during Ancient Times

**Divination in Ancient Germany**

The term Germany refers to a place where people came from Iceland and Scandinavia many centuries before the time of the Vikings. Little is only documented but thanks to the ancient Roman writers we have come to know that Ancient Germany also have use divination techniques during their time. More is known about the Vikings' practices but they represent the last survivors and practitioners of this ancient art because it was separated from the earliest Germanic times.

Divination became so firmly established in Germany during the Common Era (743 C.E.). They warned of the continuing reliance of the Germans on this ancient art despite centuries of Christian dominance. Three hundred years later, Germans forbade the practice of divination through enacting new laws. The early Germanic people saw divination as a means of determining one's fate.

Julius Caesar and Tacitus both attest to the Germanic people's faith in divination. Perhaps the thing that separate early Germanic people from other culture is that they accept women as a diviner. One of the most common techniques that Ancient Germans use for divination was casting of lots. And though much remains quite vague, we can sort of form a picture as to how they practice divination back then.

## Divination in Tibet

Those who practiced divination in Tibet are known as "mopa." Anyone could practice divination but most mopas were believed to be reincarnated lamas that are known as "tulkus." The tulkus, through repeated incarnations, were believed to have achieved great wisdom and continued to use it in the present. In our time today, the Dalai Lama is the most famous tulku alive today.

If a Tibetan desired to learn about divination and set out to become one, he/she could become a mopa. Most of these were elderly persons and also women because they were widely known for the accuracy of their readings. It wasn't uncommon back then to travel many miles just to seek advice from a highly respected diviner. There were some diviners that only practiced part – time but they are still talented individuals that can read and also rely on horoscopes.

## Chapter Two: Divination during Ancient Times

The diviners in ancient Tibet were virtually everywhere but their job only lasted depending on the accuracy of their predictions. This is why sometimes it led to an ambiguous manner wherein a mopa tend to revealed future. Symbolism is also widely used.

# Chapter Two: Divination during Ancient Times

# Chapter Three: The Art of Divination

Anyone can successfully practice the ancient art of divination. As with anything else, if divination is practiced with an open mindedness of its underlying concepts, you can gain information concerning the past and future as well as analyzing the present situation.

Divination is more of a practical art. There are just a few complex techniques that require years of study but the concepts here in this book can be done with no such exertions. With a few exceptions, the tools presented in this

## Chapter Three: The Art of Divination

book to apply divination are readily available with little to no cost at all. Before we discuss the methods, it is necessary to examine some of the finer points of the art. The next few chapters will provide you with so much information that is geared on how you can successfully apply divination.

### *The Appropriate Attitude*

Your attitude toward the practice of divination is one of the most important aspects of the art. If you only perform divination to entertain others or just for fun chances are that you will receive incorrect messages, or you will not get anything accurate simply because you are not taking the process seriously.

This is just simple logic: Why should an oracle accurately respond when the diviner himself have no sincere interest of its messages. Doubt will come in especially during the earliest stages of your divinatory work, and that's okay. You will at first have no experience that will convince you of your ability to perform divination but once you've grown comfortable with the proceedings, and perhaps have

## Chapter Three: The Art of Divination

gained true insights into the past, present and future with the use of the techniques, you will eventually and gradually replace doubt with a firm knowledge of what divination is and you will become an effective diviner.

Your attitude towards the entire process could be base on your spirituality. If you are a religious or spiritual person, you might view this ancient art as the process that reveals messages sent by the oracle or a higher force. This can also help remove any doubts concerning the viability particularly during the earliest stages of your work for divination can be seen as something of an advice and/ or supplication for guidance. This also means that even if you're not a spiritual person or you haven't practice divination, you should still respect the methods and tools being used. Just like in martial arts, the tools of combat are mysterious and because of this, deserve our respect.

Always remember that divination has frequently changed the course of history. At some point in the past, divination has helped halt battles and even toppled evil rulers. Needless to say, it has been directly or indirectly

## Chapter Three: The Art of Divination

responsible for the various ways in which numerous people have shaped their lives, and their society. So just respect the art, respect the tools and techniques used to practice it and be sincere when it comes to practicing it and be open to the responses you will received.

## *The Question*

As mentioned in the first chapter, the types of responses produce in the art of divination includes a binary or a Yes/No Response, symbolic which is the creation of symbols or images, and also selective which chooses a specific prediction. All of these can be used to answer questions. However, divination is not always performed to answer specific questions. You see, readings can be use to get a general insight into the future but of course, most of us still need a responses to the question we have. This is why questions are of utmost importance.

Questions should be carefully formulated because if the questions are not clear, then the answers produced will be vague. You should be sincere with your desire for you to

## Chapter Three: The Art of Divination

be able to receive a clear response. You also need to use common sense when asking questions. For instance, "Will I go to LA or New York next summer?" Obviously this question is not answerable by Yes or No (binary system). If you need to ask this question, it should be asked separately; "Will I go to LA this summer?" "Will I go to New York this summer?" Since the binary form is limited to answering yes or no, each of the possible choice or future event should be separately questioned.

Check out the series of questions below that's about discovering the possible whereabouts of a lost wallet. The responses are gained by using the movement of the pendulum:

Q: Is my missing wallet in the house?

A: Yes

Q: Is my wallet in the bedroom?

A: No (if it is a positive response, the following question would be skipped).

Q: Is my wallet in the living room?

## Chapter Three: The Art of Divination

A: No.

Q: Is my wallet in the couch?

A: Yes

Q: Is my wallet under the couch?

A: Yes

You see, these series of question are often needed to cover all the possible options. This kind of method has been used since the time of the Babylonians wherein the diviners spent many hours listing every possible future event that may concern the king.

The necessity of repeating this method many times in order to obtain the information needed may seem to be a great deal of work but it really requires just a little time. However, there are many methods that provide explicit answers with only one repetition.

Such question can be stated out loud, written or thought. Different techniques use different systems, and

## Chapter Three: The Art of Divination

unless the instructions are specifically states, just use what feels best.

## Repetition of Divination

In some cases, the response may be quite unclear, or you might be quite unsure of the response of the higher being. If this happens, it is always best to repeat the divination process three times. This will provide the technique the ability to maybe formulate a more comprehensible response – one that will speak to you, in order to lessen the possibility of misinterpretation.

### *Preparing Prior to Divination*

Though many forms of divination were designed in ancient times to be used at a moment's notice, some required different forms of preparation such as offerings, prayers, the burning of aromatic woods or incense, donning special garments, and bathing among others. None of this is actually necessary today but can still be used prior to performing divination rites if desired.

## Chapter Three: The Art of Divination

Such practices can calm the diviner and also allows him/her to concentrate on the question to be asked. Ritual is a process that can accomplish a specific need. In the art of divination, it usually consists of preparing the diviner for the coming act. If you feel that you need this form of pre – divinatory rite, then one of the most effective is also one that can easily be accessed. Follow the simple steps below:

- Sit quietly and breathe deeply. Make sure to not strain your breathing and just allow a relatively longer period for each time you inhale and exhale.
- Think of your question
- Do the actual technique

Most diviners agree that if circumstances allow, it is usually best to not eat a big meal prior to your divination because it is thought to desensitize the diviner – it is thought that actions like gazing is quite difficult to perform. Even with this precaution, divination should only be used when needed. No special costume is necessary like a sacred

## Chapter Three: The Art of Divination

jewelry, magical robe or a mystical headgear. Some techniques of divination are traditionally done naked but it is not really necessary. It's usually a symbolic value – that one is unafraid and unadorned and that the person is ready to receive the response given by the oracle.

## *Appropriate Times for Divination*

Ancient diviners back then do their rituals on specific natural phenomenon like the position of the planets as it is ideal for forecasting the future. Unfortunately this is highly complex because planets don't always align, and phenomena don't always happen at the moment when we need to perform divination but most importantly it's not necessary to produce a more accurate outcome.

Divination can be performed in any season, day or night. Some diviners claim that better results are acquired during a full moon and/ or waning of the moon but again it's not always necessary.

Chapter Three: The Art of Divination

*Interpreting Symbolic Responses*

If you've used a method of divination that produces symbols or images, you need to interpret them immediately after they you receive them. The diviner must then rely on his/ her own intuition in order to interpret the symbols that appeared. There are symbols that are very easy to interpret because they are crystal clear while other needs to be scrutinized closely. Try to think in symbolic ways during this important part of the rite. You need to learn how to open yourself to the answer while keeping the question in your mind. As always, if you still cannot interpret the answer, you may repeat the process until the symbols are clear to you.

**A Lack of Response**

There are times that you will feel like there aren't any responses at all even if you have already repeated the divination process. There are some forms of this art that include an option of "no answer at this time." If this happens, don't despair because a lack of response is not an

## Chapter Three: The Art of Divination

indication that you have failed. It could only mean that various energies are at work at the moment making it hard for you to come up with an accurate prediction. Should this occur, you can try doing the technique again at a later time. You see, receiving no response is much better than receiving an inaccurate response. If you want, you can also use divination to determine why there is no response that can be produce, and the answer could be enlightening to you.

# Chapter Three: The Art of Divination

## Chapter Four: Symbolic Thought

If you have the ability to read, you can already use symbolic thought. After all, printed words are nothing but strings of symbols right? – and that these words symbolize things that we generally agreed upon as a human race, or in a particular society. Therefore if we are aware of the meanings of these symbols then we can create the same interpretation just like anyone else.

A person with no knowledge of the English language would not be able to comprehend the words and that person will definitely be in the dark when it comes to the correct

## Chapter Four: Symbolic Thought

interpretation of the symbolism that each word represents. This is the same for those who are illiterate.

Symbolism had been part of our existence since the dawn of humanity, and it is perhaps the first ever language or form of communication long before the invention of any alphabet. As a matter of fact, humans have used the most graphic form of symbolism in order for them to communicate with animals and also spiritual beings. There are countless evidence that were found in walls, ceilings and floors of ancient caves all over the world. Such symbols were stunningly realistic representations of human figures as well as the animals and environment around them. Eventually, our ancestors realized that they could use images as a means of communication with other people.

Pictographs are one of the earliest forms of written speech; it is simply a stylized sketch of common objects that were used to represent physical things like household tools, plants, animals, trees, sun, moon, stars etc. There is no such thing as grammar so they only rely on these pictographs and perhaps form a connection with the images strung together and make an obscure interpretation out of it. Pictographs are

## Chapter Four: Symbolic Thought

also ideal for creating lists which obviously don't require any grammar.

Some of the earliest pictographs date as far back as 3000 B.C.E specifically in Mesopotamia. As centuries passed, the symbolism grew and it became ideographic which means it doesn't just describe an object but also the qualities that are associated with it. Thus, a pictograph of the sun can also mean light or heat. A star can also refer to the sky; a plant can also mean food or fruits.

In time, the greater symbolism that is attached to a certain pictograph the more confusing it became so the next step for our ancestors is to form a much simpler method of recording the representations of each. Pictographs were eventually stylized and altered. For instance, in Mesopotamia, a simple pictograph of the sun became a series of wedge – shaped marks that form a highly stylized symbol of it.

The symbols eventually lost the original concept, forces or ideas it resembled which is why special training in understanding and creating these signs was required and necessary so that they can understand this highly stylized

## Chapter Four: Symbolic Thought

symbols which is also known as cuneiform. Eventually they learned how to understand more complex symbolism.

As more and more culture became advanced, symbolism was then freed the restrictions of pictographs. Other complex things like ideas, emotions, deities and natural forces have also attained a symbolic form. Such symbolisms were common in religious rituals. For instance, a plow represents a grain deity while a headgear represents a war deity. Various cultures created groups of symbols that they can use in rituals, literature and also in their conversations. Our culture today for instance possesses various symbols; a heart is a symbol of love and poisonous substances have a skull and crossbones logo to indicate that it can kill a person. Colors also have symbolic value; red could mean love, stop, or even blood.

As we grow from infancy to maturity, we are eventually taught to recognize and correctly interpret these symbols. All of us are taught that symbolism has its place but the written and oral language is the ultimate form of communication. However, our ability to interpret symbols has also waned. If for instance you think: ""I don't want to

## Chapter Four: Symbolic Thought

go. I don't want to go!" it cannot be considered as symbolic thought because even if symbolism can be expressed in language, it should still consists of the recognition of non – alphabetic symbols and also their interpretation. As previously mentioned this is very important in all the symbolic forms of divination. Once you have seen symbols in a crystal sphere, clouds, fire or even a glass from which you drink this is something that's usually interpreted. This is impossible without thinking all of these objects in a symbolic way.

Sometimes, thinking in – depth is not really necessary in interpreting divinatory responses. If you have asked whether you should continue on the present path and perhaps you see an 8 – sided figure that is attached to a straight stick, it could mean that you need to "stop" or something along that line, like maybe you need to change something. However, the production of even this simple interpretation means that you need to have the ability to view the symbols in relation to the question and also find the common link though some symbolic responses may require

## Chapter Four: Symbolic Thought

more effort. You can interpret such symbols easily if you follow the techniques below:

### Look for Symbols

This is obvious but many beginners are not used to practicing it. If for instance, all you see are clouds when you look at the clouds then you are not involved in symbolic thought. Do not see the symbols merely as what they are; you need to expand your consciousness and try to see them beyond their physical structures.

### Personal Symbolism

You need to trust your instincts. For instance, if you see a cat gazing into the clouds, allow the inner meaning to come to you. If you view cats or any other animals as something loyal or faithful then their appearance can mean something positive or favorable, on the other hand, if you see them as something that terrifies you, it will surely have a different interpretation since everything is subjective.

# Chapter Four: Symbolic Thought

Most books about fortune – telling include a long list of symbols with their corresponding interpretations. However, this type of information is of little use because it is not linked with one's personal symbolic systems. Using it to predict the future can definitely cause an error, which is why you need to ignore it, or just maybe use it as a guide but you must rely on your own personal interpretation. So now the question is, how does one discover the meanings of symbols? The good thing is that you don't really need to worry about this.

The divinatory tools that you use will usually produce answers that will speak to you. You should allow yourself for these objects to speak to you after they appear so that you can interpret them in alignment with your particular question, if any. You should allow yourself to think in a symbolic way, but unfortunately science has sort of discouraged the use of this faculty because it wants us to think rationally and in a realistic way. Back then only theorists, artists, philosophers and writers are allowed to do such a thing but even them are berated for "wasting time" in superficial and borderline delusional thoughts.

## Chapter Four: Symbolic Thought

**Handling Difficulties**

There will be times when the symbols revealed will not seem to have any specific meaning. For instance, if you asked about your future love and all that you saw was a frog, you might wonder if the divination technique failed you. However, it can also be necessary to extend the symbolic thought to find its deeper meanings. In the example above, frogs can also be associated with the way they live in the wild – and usually through hopping; this symbolism may mean that you may hop from one relationship to another, or you won't settle down any time soon with a specific person.

In addition, no divination system will produce exact responses every single time. There are various factors involve that are constantly at work, which is what we mentioned in the first chapter. This uncertainty of the future may be revealed through the appearance of nonsensical symbolism. If you find that it's hard to make a link between your question and the symbolism that appeared, you can do one of two things; either do the divination technique again to clarify the response, or wait and repeat it at a later time.

# Chapter Four: Symbolic Thought

## *How You Can Develop Symbolic Thought*

You can develop symbolic thought through some exercises. It will not take much of your time but it will require your focus. You can even do this whenever you are at work, at home, while commuting or doing other things because it's just pure observation. If your eyes fall on a cup, you can use symbolic thought and try to find out what the cup might be symbolizing. Is it about waking up? Morning? Or anything else that will speak to you.

Another example is when you see a pencil, could it symbolize something about communication, creativity, or perhaps communication problem within your relationship? You see, you're not really performing any divination here but you are honing your skill to think in a more symbolic manner. If you perform the exercise above few times a day, it can definitely help you prepare your mind for symbolic thought especially during divination. Make sure to try this out as it is something that will not intrude at all into your daily life.

## Chapter Four: Symbolic Thought

There are also some people who find it hard to interpret symbols and also recognize them. If ever you are one of those, you can just practice one form of symbolic divination on a regular basis. Make sure to allow yourself to have a session every day for at least 10 to 15 minutes. As you restrain your consciousness you will eventually become aware and recognize symbols.

It's also important to note that not all forms of divination produce any symbolic response. For instance, the selective and binary systems are more straightforward. If you find it hard with having symbolic thoughts and if you have questions that concern the future, you can rely on these techniques for quite some time.

Symbolic thought is the birthright of every human being and it is something that represents an older form of human behavior wherein we go back to an age when there are just two worlds: the physical and symbolic.

# Chapter Five: The Nature of Time in Divination

The world tells us that time exists. We see the sun and how it rises and sets at specific times, and we also see seeds sprouts and how the trees lose their leaves depending on the seasons. We watch the birth and growth of a baby, and we see how clocks tick off and changes every second and minute along with the passage of days, months and years. In some Asian systems and philosophy, time is actually seen as a form of illusion like everything else. It is true that we need to have a concept of time because it keeps our lives orderly and practical – we can go to bed at night with the knowledge

## Chapter Five: The Nature of Time in Divination

that upon waking up it wouldn't be ten years earlier but just a day later. Using these examples, time is viewed as a form of convenient tool that we can use to organize our existence but in reality there is no such thing as time.

Even if you view it at the simplest level, one's perception of time is quite confusing. You see, when you first read the book, it was the present and that moment now is in the past. You are now currently experiencing a new present as you read this sentence, and the future is but a moment away. Time is neither a universal law nor a physical phenomenon such as gravity. Time only consists of our perception of what seems to be a natural phenomenon. Any book that discusses divination would be incomplete if the concepts of time as well as its theories are not discussed.

This is what this chapter is all about. You will learn the most commonly accepted ideas that determine whether they are supported by divination's practice, and ends with the most useful way of time's concepts. Thinking about time in a different way than how a normal person perceives it is very important to a diviner. You must learn how to view

## Chapter Five: The Nature of Time in Divination

time from a larger and less physical base so that you'll be successful in looking at the past, present and future.

The most common explanation of time is that it consists of a one way stream. Our birth puts us into that concept of one way stream. We sit facing downstream wherein we are able to see the past to gain knowledge of the present but unable to look behind us to predict the future. We continue our journey until we "die" or leave this plane of existence. This theory does not really support the art of divination and it is because it states that we can never know the future because it simply has not happened yet.

There is a related theory that again sees time as a stream. If you go on a boat and float down the river while directing where to go, the strong current tend to make us move forward but through effort, we can travel upstream and revisit the places we have been or even jump ahead for short periods just to see what lies around the bend of the river. This allows the diviner to have some flexibility to perceive the future but it still sees time as a linear phenomenon which is why it is again not suited to the practice of divination just like the first theory.

## Chapter Five: The Nature of Time in Divination

The third theory of time is like that a book. For instance, you can start reading the first chapter and continue to the end but it is perfectly possible to look in advance and read how the story will end – future. The theory is based upon the assumption that the future is already written. This concept supports the practice of divination but divination itself doesn't support it because this theory depends on the concept of destiny and fate.

The fourth concept is almost poetic. It states that time is spiral and has always existed – that one's life leads to the center, and there is already a set path for all of us. We can jump from one part of the spiral to the next to see what has been or what will be and still be able to return to the now. This theory is also based on fate or pre – destination which is why it also does not fit the definition of divination.

However, some believe that time itself is more complex than any of the theories you have just read. Time is not linear or it doesn't go into a straight motion but of all motions in all directions – be it spiral, circle, curve, zigzag etc. It is this activity that is responsible for our perception of the past, present and future.

## Chapter Five: The Nature of Time in Divination

Time is seen as a dimension that intersects with our physical world, and that it is something that can be measured and also bring order to our lives but does not in any way control it. Just like what Albert Einstein said, time is something that prevents everything from happening at once. If you view time in this way, the past, present and future don't exist but it also simultaneously exists. Again, time is a perception of events as happening yesterday, today or tomorrow that provides a structure on which to build our lives.

In the first chapter, you have learned how the energy that radiates from the past and present can somehow shape the future. For you to better understand it, think of yourself as standing in the center of a large plain. There are many paths that stretch out from where you are standing, each representing the past or a possible future. The position that you occupy is the present moment. This means that we can look down the roads that we have been before at this time and through examining them; you can determine which of the future paths you will likely take. This is exactly how the process of divination is all about – it's about finding the most plausible path. However, one can alter the future

## Chapter Five: The Nature of Time in Divination

through taking an alternate path but all of which leads to the same destination which is the future present.

As you now have learned, it is virtually impossible to discuss divination without referring to terms like past, present and future. Our perception of time is a valuable ally in our lives because it allows us to view them as a linear experience even though we know that it is not. To return to our earlier image of time, we are all standing in the middle of all the paths, walking toward the center and also simultaneously traveling away from it. If you find the information in this chapter to be quite confusing, keep in mind that a few people other than physicists and philosophers ever dwell on time's nature. We have all been taught that time operated in one manner which allows us to live our live in a more structure and organized manner.

To summarize, time is an illusion but it is an extremely valuable illusion. Divination offers a means of going beyond the constraints of time and allows an individual to see the past, present and future. Keep in mind that the present is in the past and that the future is already here now.

## Chapter Six: Altering Your Future

One of the most common misunderstandings when it comes to divination is the belief that it will reveal our entire destiny. This is just incorrect because in divination, the future is something that can still be changed. This is what we have discussed in the last few chapters, and it is also something that was first discovered by our ancestors who are practicing it. Even in religious doctrines, we are regarded as possessing free will which means we have the power to alter the future.

## Chapter Six: Altering Your Future

As what we have mentioned in the second chapter of this book, the Babylonians has a firm belief that they could alter the future by using specialized prayers and rituals to their deities. This concept is also shared by numerous ancient cultures.

Obviously, it would be great if the response of every divination practice is something positive; if the reading reveals anything that relates to us being totally at peace, happy, loved, fulfilled, and prosperous in the future wherein nothing dangerous, negative or harmful will come our way. However, we all know that this rarely happens simply because we are mere mortals – we make mistakes, we let others lead us to dark paths; we rely on emotions when we need to think, or use our brains when we need to feel. No human life can completely avoid the bumps and failures that lie on the road. Overcoming them and dealing with these challenges, whether we like it or not, are part of our daily existence.

It is true that trials are often balanced with triumphs, losses with gains, and broken relationships with more successful ones. Divination has the ability to forecast not just

## Chapter Six: Altering Your Future

the joy but also the pain. The latter is what the next section is all about. You see, our futures are not pre – set plans, for we create it with every choice we make.

## Karma

There are some people that accept the doctrine of karma, and maybe they also wonder how we can escape its (negative) effects. Since karma is a widely accepted concept today, it's essential to discuss it from the viewpoint of divination. So how does karma affect the future?

Karma is usually described as a phenomenon or an event that can directly influence our lives. Most people believe that past action particularly the negative one will come back to them through a process so mysterious only little is understood. It became an illustration of cause and effect. If we make mistakes, we will receive lessons in the future that will enable us to avoid the same mistake. These lessons can take the form of problems that we otherwise wish to avoid.

## Chapter Six: Altering Your Future

Some even say that the effects of karma are inescapable – it's like a "universal police" a law that you can't get away with. There are also those who think that even the actions we took in our previous lives can return to haunt us and catch up with our present lives.

Many people see the concept of karma as a type of universal teacher wherein we should show up in order to learn the right behavior. According to this viewpoint, part of our future is perhaps pre – determined by our own choices and actions. Some people use divination in order to reveal these karmic debts. And once they are aware of the problem, then they can take the necessary action. If these people followed the teaching analogy we used earlier, then it means that these diviners do their homework so that the next challenge will be of minimal pain, and even if they don't totally escape karma's effects, they can still work with the process.

Karmic lessons can be viewed as the event when the energy waves that we radiated before was returned to us. Thus, just like our futures, we create karma on a daily basis through our own choices and actions. We may not be able to

## Chapter Six: Altering Your Future

fully escape being faced with all its lessons but if we do the right thing and perhaps make our current behavior better, we may avoid future tragedies, challenges or be able to handle painful situations well through having a positive outlook. Karmic lessons are also seen as some predictions of the future. It functions as a warning for us to learn the lesson now and take action so that it can minimize the impact in the future.

## *Action and Thought to Prevent Negative Future Events*

There is no time like now to start reshaping your future. The exact techniques of accomplishing this largely rely on the nature of the forewarning received though the following advice may be used with minor adaptations so that it can help in dealing with any type of warnings.

Warnings are usually concerned with very important matters so whenever you receive one during divination, you need to always double – check it to ensure that there is no error in the method or interpretation that has created such response. Check out the tips on the next page.

Chapter Six: Altering Your Future

### Retrain Your Mind

You need to focus on a positive future. It is true that we cannot live a life with zero problems, but one should never think about the negative response. You need to learn how to block it out of existence and do not even consider it as something inescapable.

### Use other divination methods

You need to use the most effective technique in order to create the change. Methods that produce yes or no answers are usually advisable as there is less room for erroneous interpretations, unless of course, the divination rites are incorrectly performed.

### Work at solving one problem at a time

If you are faced with many warnings, choose the most negative then once you have achieved the needed changes that is determined through divination, you should take a rest and start to work on much lesser problems but at a later date.

## Chapter Six: Altering Your Future

**Act in accordance with your need**

For instance, if you have foreseen that a planned move will cause you illness, financial loss or heartache, you can take the necessary steps now to change your plans if you want to avoid it in the near future. If you see trouble that concerns the relationship you are in now, then you can start re – examining your feelings toward that special someone. Communicate more, lay everything out to him/ her or do what needs to be done because some relationships need real hard work for it to be emotionally fulfilling to both parties. Never allow the warning to be manifested.

Another example is if sickness is foretold, you can start changing the pattern of your life. Make sure to get regular and non – intensive exercise, watch your diet and eat healthier foods, or perhaps cultivate a positive outlook in life. Stress has been clinically proven to bring about illnesses, which is why you should do something to help reduce stress in your life. You can also start breaking life – draining habits that do not benefit you. Then, after releasing the fear, you should do daily affirmations in order to celebrate the coming positive changes as well as to strengthen both your conscious and subconscious mindset. It doesn't have to be a long sentence; in fact, the shorter it is, the easier it can be memorized. Some may find it hard to accomplish genuine change because many of us are simply stubborn. We usually don't like change and we tend to follow a preset plan. These feelings should be released if you want to be successful at altering your future. You need to be more flexible and see the positive side of every challenge or problems that come your way.

## **Take responsibility for your life**

You need to realize that no higher being has predetermined the course of anyone's life, and that's because of free will. This only means that you are totally responsible and you need to assume this task and not let other adversely affect your life. You need to be deliberate and also learn to forgive yourself for the mistake you will make. Release the negativity so that you can start creating a more favorable future.

# Chapter Seven: Advance Technique Part I

The Lien Shan is said to have begun with the hexagram Kên (Keeping Still), and the Kuei Ts'ang began with the hexagram called K'un (The Receptive). According to historians, they cannot tell whether the names of the 64 hexagrams being followed today are used back then, and if so, whether they are the same structure that's now present in the Book of Changes. The I Ching is an elegant system of divination. Re - publication of the book during the late 1960s and early 1970s created intense interest in its use.

## Chapter Seven: Advance Techniques Part I

### *The Book of Changes in Divination*

The Book of Changes is authored by four teachers namely, Confucius, Fu Hsi, the Duke of Chou, and King Wên. Fu Hsi is one of the earliest legendary figures in China; he is known as the creator of the linear symbols of Book of Changes or the Book of Changes during the period when men is still hunting and fishing for a living. This means that the signs or meaning are so ancient that it occurred before any historical memory. Furthermore, the eight trigrams have names that aren't linked to any forms of Chinese language, and because of this people thought that the names originated from a foreign language. The trigrams are not also identified as archaic characters even if some people thought that it has some kind of resemblance among ancient Chinese characters.

The eight trigrams are found to be occurring in different combinations during the early times. Two book collections that are considered as a relic are namely, the Book of Changes of the Hsia dynasty known as the Lien

# Chapter Seven: Advance Techniques Part I

Shan, and the Book of Changes of the Shang dynasty known as Kuei Ts'ang.

## *The Yin and Yang*

The Yin and Yang symbol has become a significant principle especially in India as well as in Europe. However, the gnostic – dualistic concept are not align to the original idea of the Book of Changes because what Yin and Yang suggests is simply the ridgepole (t'ai chi) or the line. The line represents oneness, duality comes into the world, and the line creates a world of opposites (an above and below; forward and backward; right and left etc.)

The duality concept of the Yin and Yang became popular especially during the transition period of the Ch'in and Han dynasties in China; these dynasties were the time period before our era. It was the time when every student or person carries the doctrine of Yin and Yang. It became the notion, and it became a very important principle to live by.

## Chapter Seven: Advance Techniques Part I

At the time, the Book of Changes or Book of Changes was use as a book of magic; the students read concepts that are not originally in the book. The Yin and Yang doctrine has naturally attracted the attention of foreigners outside of China since the primal principles it that of a male and female (duality).

Some philosophers compared the Yin concept as "the overcast" or "the cloudy" while the Yang is a "banner that's waving in the sun," "bright," "shining." The duality concepts were also explained as the dark and light sides of a river or a mountain. In the case of a mountain, the southern part is the brighter side while the northern area is the darker side. Similarly, in the case of the river, if it was seen from a bird's point – of – view, the southern side is in the shadow (yin), while the northern side where the light is being reflected is the bright side (yang). The duality concepts were carried over to the Book of Changes, and were applied to the two alternating primal states of being. It's important to note though that the Yin and Yang don't occur in such derived

# Chapter Seven: Advance Techniques Part I

sense either in the old commentaries or in the actual book itself.

The dual concept first occurred in the Great Commentary, which already shows influence from Taoism. In the Commentary on the Decision, yin and yang weren't used instead it was referred to as "the yielding," and "the firm" respectively. Do take note that whatever terms are applied to these dual concepts, it is certain that the world of being arises out of interplay. Thus change is conceived as a continuous transformation of a force into the other and also as a cycle of phenomena where they themselves are connected such as summer and winter, day and night. Therefore, change is not meaningless; it is subject to tao or the universal law.

## The Theory of Ideas

The second fundamental concept in the Book of Changes is its theory of ideas. The 8 trigrams are images that aren't so much of objects as of states of changes. This view is

## Chapter Seven: Advance Techniques Part I

linked with the concepts that Lao – tse and Confucius taught to their students in their oral teachings – that every manifestation in the visible and physical world is the effect of an "image," vision or an idea of the unseen world or spiritual realm. Accordingly, everything that happens in our world is only a reproduction or perhaps a reflection of the events that we perceive or expect it to be which is beyond our sense of perception.

The holy men and sages who are aligned or who can communicate with such higher realms or levels of the unseen world gain access to ideas through using their intuition making them able to intervene or decisively take part in the manifestation of events in the world. Thus man is linked with heaven and with the earth - the world of ideas and the material world form a trinity of primal powers.

The theory of seen and unseen ideas is applied in a twofold sense; the Book of Changes shows the image of events as well as the unfolding of the conditions. If one will discern and reflect upon it to create a better decision in the present moment, one must learn to foresee the future and to

## Chapter Seven: Advance Techniques Part I

also understand the past. In this way, the images or symbolism on which the hexagrams are based will serve as the pattern for what one should do in a certain situation. The Great Commentary doesn't only adapt the course of nature that's made possible but it also attempts to trace the origin of all the inventions and practices of mankind to archetypal ideas and images. Even if the hypothesis can or cannot be applied to specific circumstances, it still contains a certain truth.

### *The Judgments*

The third element that's fundamental to the Book of Changes is the judgments. The judgments interpret the images in the hexagram, and it indicates whether a given action will bring fortune or misfortune as well as humiliation or remorse. The judgments help a man when it comes to making a decision to desist from a course of action that's indicated by the circumstance of the moment but could not be beneficial or perilous in the long term. In this way, one makes himself independent of the tyranny of

## Chapter Seven: Advance Techniques Part I

situations. The judgments and interpretations open to the readers and students the richest treasure of Chinese wisdom. A person can have a comprehensive knowledge and view of human experience through it as this can enable a person to shape his/ her life according to his own will and accord it or align it with the ultimate universal law of tao.

The Book of Changes' ethical and intellectual guidance can be unlocked through a general perusal of the texts within each chapter. A person can also consult and seek guidance from the Book of Changes to provide answers to personal questions or bring a person closer to the truth that he/ she is trying to find. Since Book of Changes is a book of universal wisdom, it will always give the seeker appropriate answers provided that one follows the rules dictated by the book's structure.

In order for a seeker to effectively use the Book of Changes as a guide to answer specific questions, one must learn to adapt the question to the structure established by the book which is the Yin and Yang doctrine. The book will only answer questions in a dualistic approach wherein there

## Chapter Seven: Advance Techniques Part I

will be two alternatives and each one requires a different action.

It's important to note that when a seeker is consulting the Book of Changes for answers or guidance, the seeker should only create a question that are answerable by the two paths or possibilities since it follows the Yin and Yang doctrine. If used properly, the Book of Changes will offer concrete answers to the right questions, and it will always lead the seeker to the right course of action.

## How to Use the Book of Changes

For instance, you are facing with the dilemma of accepting a job offer in another country which could mean that you need to decide whether or not you'd be willing to leave your home. If you ask it in this way: "Should I accept the job offer in another country or should I just stay in my home country?" The Book of Changes won't yield you an answer. You must formulate the question like this "Should I accept the job offer in another country?" or, "Should I stay in

## Chapter Seven: Advance Techniques Part I

my home country?" As you can see, if you formulate the question this way, the Book of Changes can ultimately guide you and provide an answer because it's answerable by either a negative or a positive which is what the Yin and Yang doctrine is all about.

The Book of Changes answer to the properly formulated question aforementioned may warn you that at the moment, you lack the needed endurance or experience to undertake a specific path, and that it would be risky to embark on a particular course without first acquiring more experience or building strength. By illuminating the outcome of every foreseeable situation, the Book of Changes will guide a person to become mindful of the steps that one must take before doing anything or acting in a particular path. It will also guide a seeker on how to undertake and successful complete a specific endeavor so that even if there are difficulties or obstructions along the way, the action that one will take remains favorable.

## Chapter Seven: Advance Techniques Part I

The Book of Changes astonishingly accurate answers to people's queries are not a mystery because the book is based on the principle of objectivity. Usually when a person is facing hardships and have no clue on what to do, they seek a trustworthy person or perhaps a trusted confidant to ask for advice; this could be a friend, mentor, parent, leader etc. People generally tend to do that because one's subjectivity doesn't allow a person to view a problem with a clear mind, and this is usually because our emotions are entangled with the problem which is why it obscures reality.

Whenever we explain a certain problem to a trustworthy confidant, usually two operative factors happen that makes a person arrive towards a possible solution; first, we must clearly explain the problem and provide elaborate details as well as the possible outcomes thereby further clarifying the conflict for ourselves. Second, that person will now consider the problem from another angle and can therefore provide perhaps a more objective opinion. The combination of the clear explanation and the objective opinion of your trustworthy confidant may help resolve the

## Chapter Seven: Advance Techniques Part I

problem but keep in mind that even if we seek guidance or advice from others, the answer is already within us it's just that most times we don't have a clear mind to be able to 'see' it.

If you start to see the problem in a more objective way, you can then start to open up and accept external guidance that will help and lead you in finding the right answers or taking the right course.

The Book of Changes answers a seeker's question in a similar manner. When a person learns how to externalize the problem in a form of question, the Book of Changes will make you better understand your situation, and you'll be able to accept the logic behind Book of Changes's answer. If you accept it, you can be guided accordingly. The gift of Book of Changes is that it helps people to view their circumstances with objectivity so that one can take the right action to achieve a desired outcome.

## Chapter Seven: Advance Techniques Part I

You can choose to consult the Book of Changes as a general book of wisdom or you can also use it to seek guidance through posing the appropriate question and answer system that is align with how the book is structured. In either case, you'll learn from its images, and you'll be guided by the principles and ethics which will further enrich your life and elevate you as a human being who can be of better service to your society.

# Chapter Seven: Advance Techniques Part I

# Chapter Eight: Advance Techniques Part II

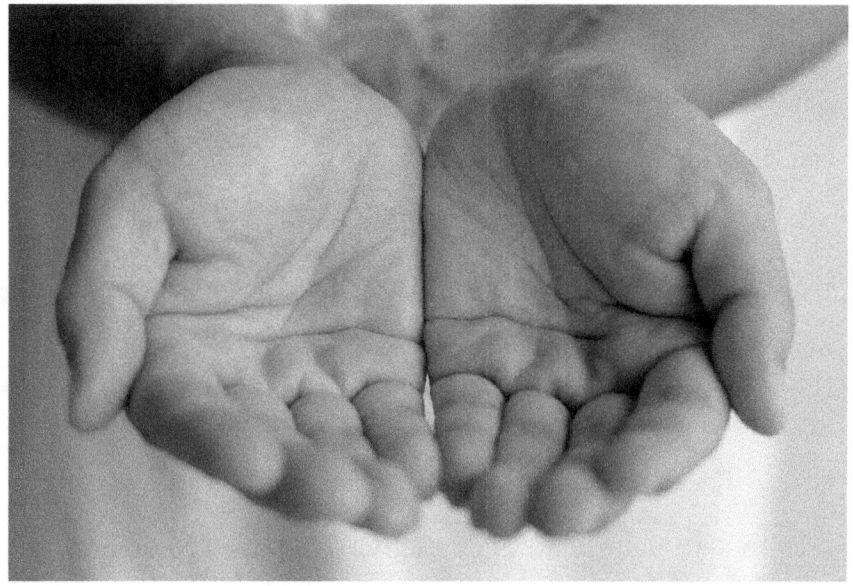

Palm reading dates back to the first human civilization. There were a lot of hand paintings found in prehistoric caves during the Stone Age. The art of palm reading were also found in Vedic scripts, Vedic bible and also early Semitic writings. Aristotle even suggested that there's a connection in the long lines of palm with the gods. However, because of the rise of Christianity, palmistry and other practices similar to it has been viewed as heresy because it lacks factual basis and it is simply not a sound or believable concept.

## Chapter Eight: Advance Techniques Part II

### *Chiromancy in Divination*

Chiromancy is the study and interpretation of the human palms. Palmist or palm readers basically look at the hands of their subjects or customers and perform a thorough analysis of the many aspects of the hand, and from there draws hypothetical meanings in accordance to the rules and structure of palmistry.

There are many factors to consider before one can do a proficient palm reading; usually, experts try to determine first the nature of the person they're trying to read. It involves learning about the subject's character, personality, mentality, physical aspects, sexuality, and background as well as other essential factors such as the complexity and characteristics of the hand and fingers.

Every hand is unique, and it tells a different story. Just like fingerprints, you can never find the exact same hand print because every individual who ever lived is quite 'special,' perhaps it is what makes us human. There may be

## Chapter Eight: Advance Techniques Part II

some similarities in terms of patterns but it's not the same. Even if individuals have the exact same hand print, for sure, they still came from different backgrounds and have different set of personalities which will alter the meaning of their palms altogether.

Each pair of hands for one individual is also unique; you don't get the exact same hand print for both your left and right hands, which is why it should also be treated individually. If a palmist says that they can predict when an individual is going to get married and have kids, or when will someone dies they are most likely a fraud or a *charlatan* because they have lost touched with reality and became too idealistic already. A true palmist or a proficient reader should not claim anything; you can quickly tell or gauge if they're proficient or not by the number of years they've been in the field or by how well they assess everything before making any assumptions – not conclusions.

Despite of palmistry's long history, it is still fairly new and still has lots of aspects yet to be discovered. Some

## Chapter Eight: Advance Techniques Part II

experts say that palmistry can be used to treat psychological illnesses or mental issues because the nature of its process involves exploring a person's inner self to reveal one's conflicts and draw 'predictions' from there. It's almost the same with what psychologist or mental therapist do to a patient in order for him/her to get in touch with his/her inner self to resolve underlying issues. Palmistry could be one of the treatments that could help in curing psychiatric illnesses in the future according to some experts.

Time can only tell if palmistry can be proven as a valuable tool in the field of psychiatric medicine, and will one day be part of psychology's future. It's still a long way before that can happen, but like any other things, it can be a possibility. Nevertheless, if you are interested in delving into the unknown, and grapple with human nature's complexities then palmistry can help you get started.

# Chapter Eight: Advance Techniques Part II

## *Physical Factors*

Before getting to the basics of palm reading, here's a brief outline of the factors that you're going to have to deal with to aid you in reading hand prints accurately.

- Skin texture in palmistry refers to the innate degree of refinement. You can gauge one's skin texture by looking at the back of your subject's hand. You will need to determine the texture of the person you're reading to be able to give an accurate interpretation.

- Determining the palm color will indicate the vitality and warmth of your subject.

- The consistency of the hand indicates the energy level of your customer. You can determine the 'fullness' or 'nothingness' of life of the person you're reading through feeling his/her hand and noting the degree of its elasticity or the ability of the body to recover its shape after being deformed. If the hand has a springiness quality to it, it is elastic.

# Chapter Eight: Advance Techniques Part II

- This may be hard to fathom especially for beginners. Having a flexible hand usually indicates the degree of mental flexibility of an individual as well as its adaptability to be open to new ideas and circumstances.
- The length of a person's finger usually indicates the degree of thought that your customer is likely to give in a particular matter, or how deep they delve into a certain subject that attracts their attention.
- The finger knots indicate the thinking process of an individual. It's either a cover smooth type or knotty fingers.
- The finger phalanges deal with a person's mind and a particular matter that he/she is most concerned with. It could be his/her family life, her marriage, her relationships, her career etc.
- The shape of a person's fingertip is an indicator of a person's mental outlook.
- Thumbs are classified into different types just like the size of the hand and the fingers. Studying the thumb will

# Chapter Eight: Advance Techniques Part II

make a palmist get a clear insight of his/her subject's character or personality.

- o The mounts (which will be discussed later in this book) will enable a palmist to determine your subject's deepest desires, their passion and what they truly want in life.

## *Active vs. Passive Zones*

There is also the so - called active and passive zones in the hand which will help a palmist understand if the subject likes to make things happen or just let circumstances happen to them.

The first you need to determine before reading a palm is if your subject is left or right handed. After which you have to examine both hands before making any conclusions or determining which hand you will settle with to perform a reading. The standard meaning of the two hands is that the "active hand" or the hand that does most of the work is the part that records the present, while the "passive hand" usually records the qualities the subject was born with – or

## Chapter Eight: Advance Techniques Part II

who you are by default, you can say that this is an individual's baseline before the brain made assumptions about the person's future. Most people are right handed (active hand), while the left hand is the passive one; for left handed people, it's just vice – versa.

However, if that is the case then the passive hand is unlikely to change since it's something that you are born with, so it's probably better to say that the passive hand indicates qualities and an individual's disposition after he/she finished laying out the foundations of his/her life.

Most psychologists agree that it is during our childhood where we lay life's foundation to aid us as we grow old. The decisions, choices, conclusions, assumptions we made during our formative years affects how we will live as adults, this includes how we deal with other people and our inner self as well as how we look at the world where we live. These are the basis of the person we will eventually become, thus the difference of the two hands – the passive hand indicates subconscious levels of who we were when our biological system changed as we go from one phase to

## Chapter Eight: Advance Techniques Part II

another, while the active hand indicates the outer and more conscious selves, and how a person have develop and evolved from that point.

Comparing both hands will determine your subject's progression and development over the years, whether they developed in a positive or negative way. If the prints of both hands are somewhat similar, then it could be an indication that an individual just sort of went with the flow with whatever disposition or talent they were given when their childhood was over.

If the active hand shows negative prints than the passive hand, it indicates that they fell to the many temptations given before them, and perhaps failed to make use of their talents and capabilities after their childhood stage. If the active hand shows more positive prints than the passive one, then that means that an individual made an effort to enhance his/her given talent and build something from whatever they started during their youth. Sometimes this development came about because of necessity but other times it is a person's own choice.

# Chapter Eight: Advance Techniques Part II

A change in the formation of hand prints are very rare, but if ever you come across with something like that, it only goes to show that drastic changes have been made by that person particularly his/her inner being and subconscious as well the foundation laid during his/her childhood. It is also most likely that the person also altered the values or ideas he/she had cherished ever since. This could likely happen if the person underwent a very traumatic event that led him/her to change his/her core values and foundation.

## Texture of Palm

The first ever step in becoming a palm reader is to check the quality of your subject's skin. In this book, the texture will be divided into seven groups: extremely – fine, fine, medium – fine, medium, medium – coarse, coarse, and extremely coarse. So that beginners can easily grasp the concept and also be able to classify the texture of the palms that one will encounter. Assessing the texture of your skin is

## Chapter Eight: Advance Techniques Part II

essential to learn about your subject's natural degree of innate personality.

Basically, the finer the texture the more sophisticated a person is. It means that they are more sensitive, and their attitude or feelings can be easily disturbed by something that emotionally upsets them. If the person has a rougher and coarser skin texture that usually indicates that he/she is more basic, and down – to – earth kind of person. These kinds of people are simple and can't be affected easily by circumstances that happen to them.

In the next section you'll be given a quick and easy to read overview of each skin texture so you can easily classify the kind of hand your reading.

- Extremely – fine skin texture palm. These kinds of hand texture are extremely rare. Aside from being fine, it is also very soft and delicate which indicates that they are very sophisticated in nature, and they get easily upset when a situation offends their inner

## Chapter Eight: Advance Techniques Part II

sense or refinement. These people tend to love fine or delicate things and dislike anything that is vulgar or brutal because it could somehow cause them pain.

- Fine - skin texture. This is one of the most common skin textures you will encounter. It's almost the same with extremely – fine texture. These kinds of people like to hang – out with equally sophisticated people. They tend to respect more down – to – earth people like those who are in entry – level jobs or something similar but they may not find it easy or enjoy their company in a social situation.

- Medium – fine skin texture. It indicates your subject is well balanced in their attitude between that which is down – to – earth and that which is refined or sophisticated person. Since it is still classified as medium – fine these kinds of people is still refined in nature.

## Chapter Eight: Advance Techniques Part II

- Medium - skin texture. These kinds of palms are also rare, not a lot of experts use this kind of classification. It can be hard to identify but medium skin texture has certain elasticity to it. People who possess a medium skin texture often strike a balance between sophistication and basic.

- Medium - coarse skin texture. Easily recognizable and could be encountered frequently. Even if there's a certain sense of coarseness to it, it still isn't coarse enough to be classified as rough. Usually indicates being well – balanced but has an inclination towards earthiness.

- Coarse - skin texture. Usually recognizable because the skin on the back of the hand looks rough and leathery and indicates a person who is inclined to be simple, uncomplicated and also down – to – earth nature. These kinds of people are usually not interested in the subtleties of life, and have a strong dislike for anything they see as being pretentious.

- Extremely - coarse skin texture. This is also very rare to find, similar to extremely fine texture. It is easily recognizable as the skin on the back of the hand looks very rough and coarse looks like extremely low grade leather. It is usually found on the kinds of people that have primitive lifestyles. People with this texture are primitive in their innate nature and also indifferent to any form of sophistication or what they consider as pretentious. These kinds of people are so uncomplicated, very simple and cannot understand the complexities of modern society; perhaps they are also very practical.

*Consistency*

The consistency of the hand along with skin texture, palm color and flexibility can help any practitioner read the palms better because it gives a huge amount of information. In fact, according to many experts even if you have limited knowledge of palmistry and you can only rely on skin texture, consistency, flexibility, and color, you can still be

## Chapter Eight: Advance Techniques Part II

capable of doing accurate and in-depth readings! This is how important these factors are!

Hand consistency is determined by taking your subject's hand and then exerting a gentle pressure to see how elastic the flesh is. Try shaking their hand for you to get the idea. You should also get your subject to stretch out their hand and try pressing into the flesh of the palm with the ball of your thumb to see how much resistance there is. Just like the skin texture, hand consistency can be classified to many types namely; very hard, hard, elastic-hard, elastic, elastic-soft, soft, and very soft and flabby.

In the next section you'll be given a quick and easy to read overview of each types of hand consistency so you can easily classify your subject's hand.

- Very Hard Hands: These are very rare to find, and certainly has extreme indications. Virtually has no elasticity, and can be hard to press or squeeze. Usually indicates that your subject is a very energetic

## Chapter Eight: Advance Techniques Part II

person, extremely active and always ready to do anything he/she could possibly do. These kinds of people lack intelligence and often times they could be working at something without giving any real thought.

- Hard Hands: Frequently found compared to very hard hands category. Also quite recognizable because you can squeeze their hand or press it but there's just little give to it. However, there's a sign of elasticity. Almost has similar traits with very hard hands, the only difference perhaps is that they are not quite as mindless in the way they spend their energy.

- Elastic Hard Hands: Has the kind of hand that has a degree of elasticity enough to prevent it from being classified as hard. Usually indicate that your subject is full of energy but it is intelligently directed.

- Elastic Hands: Has certain firmness and quite difficult to press but once you let go the flesh bounces back

## Chapter Eight: Advance Techniques Part II

like a rubber ball. Usually indicates that the person also has a huge amount of energy but also intelligent in the way they do things. They work hard and they work smart; keeping in mind what they're doing and don't want to waste their energy into something useless. They are also full of life but they're quite balance. It's usually found in successful people as well.

- Elastic Soft Hands: Even if the hands are elastic, you can easily recognize or differentiate it because there is certain softness to the flesh, it doesn't bounce back like the elastic hands. Usually, it indicates that a person is willing to work very hard to get what they want. They are the kind of people that have a sense of laziness but their sometimes it overrides their desire to work. It also goes to show that the person enjoys working as much as they enjoy other pleasures. They tend to seek a job that can be enjoyable but not too mentally or physically demanding.

# Chapter Eight: Advance Techniques Part II

- Soft Hands: Very recognizable because it is very soft once pressed and lacks elasticity. Usually indicates that a person is lazy and likes to indulge on certain things too much. It's usually has all the skill and intelligence but lacks effort.

- Very Soft and Flabby Hands: These are extreme indications and also very recognizable because once you squeeze the hand it looks like their flesh want to ooze out! It also indicated that the person is more of a dreamer and not a doer. Don't usually make an effort to materialize their ideas or dreams.

## *Hand Flexibility*

The flexibility of the hand indicates the versatility of your subject's mind and their ability to adapt their mentality to new and progressive ideas, new ways of doing things, and changing circumstances.

The rule of thumb for flexibility is that the more flexible the hand, the more flexible the mentality. To gauge

# Chapter Eight: Advance Techniques Part II

the degree of flexibility you should hold the tips of your subject's fingers in one hand support the wrist with the other and then exert a gentle pressure until you have bent the hand back as far as it will go. Be careful not to hurt your subject!

## *The Mounts*

There are seven mounts on the hand namely; Mount of Jupiter, Saturn, Apollo, Mercury, Moon, Venus, and Mount of Mars. Each of which indicates a particular aspect of a subject's nature. The job of the palm reader is to decide on the relative strength of each mount, pick the strongest or most dominating area, and then arrange other mounts into their order of prominence. In this section, you'll be provided with some basic interpretations about each mounts.

It's also recommended that you study the areas of each mounts so that you can be familiar of its locations in the palm.

- Mount of Jupiter: There are four fingers underneath each of which is a mount. Under the first or index

## Chapter Eight: Advance Techniques Part II

finger is the Mount of Jupiter which indicates the person's desire to have a control over their life and those who affect it. If the mount of Jupiter is prominent it means that your subject possess a leadership quality. It is an indicator that the person is honest and optimistic. However, if it is flat that means that he/she lacks confidence, and if the mount is over – developed (or really dominant over others) it's an indicator that the person is egoistic and arrogant.

- Mount of Saturn: The mount of Saturn is located under the second or middle finger. It indicates a desire for stability and security. It also means that the person is very responsible and seeks wisdom. If the mount is flat, the person could be optimistic and loves to socialize. However, if it is overdeveloped and your subject possess a long finger, it's an indicator that he/she is an introvert or quite distant to people.

- Mount of Apollo: It is located under the third or ring finger and usually indicates the desire to express

## Chapter Eight: Advance Techniques Part II

one's own individuality or personal uniqueness. If the mount is well – developed, the person is quite optimistic and warm but if it is flat, it usually means that he/she is cynical and cold.

- Mount of Mercury: It is located under the fourth or little finger and usually indicates the desire to communicate. These are the kinds of people who loves to travel and is a go – getter. However, if the mount of Mercury is overdeveloped that indicates the person is a liar. A flat mount means that he/she is often shy and boring.

- Mount of Moon or Mount of Luna: Located at the base of the palm across the thumb, if it is well – developed it usually means that the person is compassionate, loving, creative and also enthusiastic about life but if it is flat, it indicates a sense of empathy and also good imagination.

## Chapter Eight: Advance Techniques Part II

- Mount of Venus: Can be found under the thumb, and usually indicates that the degree of generosity and warmness. If it is well – developed it means that they are an interesting companion and leads a social life. If the mount of Venus is overdeveloped it shows that he/she is greedy and wants to acquire material things, and if it is flat that means that your subject lacks passion and he/she is also selfish.

- Mount of Mars: The Mount of Mars which is divided into two zones; active and passive; underneath the Mount of Jupiter and inside the Life Line is the Mount of Lower Mars which indicates the person's desire to push or force their way forward in life. Across the hand is the Mount of Upper Mars which indicates their desire to stick to their resolutions and persist in their endeavors.

# Chapter Nine: Advance Techniques Part III

Though the precise origins of both playing cards and the Tarot are unknown, no cards have survived from truly ancient cultures. The Tarot-a deck of cards used in divination is of fairly recent origin, perhaps during the 13th century in Europe. It is also likely that, far from a mysterious origin, the Tarot was invented for educational Christian purposes, for gambling, or for pure amusement. Divinatory practices with the Tarot were a later development.

# Chapter Nine: Advance Techniques Part III

## *Tarot in Divination*

The tarot deck is made up of 78 cards that are divided into two sections – the major arcana and the minor. Arcana or Arcanum means "profound secrets" according to the alchemists from the Middle Ages. They believe that the tarot cards are a collection of these 'secrets' that explains the nature, life, unconscious mind and the universe.

The Major Arcana consist of 22 cards and they are considered as the "heart of the deck." These cards also represent sort of the 'bigger picture' during reading. It mostly symbolizes some kind of inherent aspect of human experience or patterns that influences human nature. The major arcana is given utmost importance during a tarot reading since these cards represent a person's most basic concerns and often times involves the spiritual aspect and inner self. It starts from the card of beginnings called The Fool (0) and ends in a card called The World (22).

The numbers also correspond and are correlated with the numbers of the cards in the minor arcana. The Minor Arcana is composed of 56 cards which are divided into four

## Chapter Nine: Advance Techniques Part III

suits – the Wands, Cups, Swords and Pentacles. Each of the suits also has Court Cards (The Page, The Knight, The Queen and The King) and Pip Cards that are numbered from 1 to 10. The minor arcana deals with a more universal and practical theme, its concern about the emotions, struggles and events of the day to day life of an individual. In the next section, you'll see the meanings, words, and interpretations of each card in the major and minor arcana as well as the general meaning of each suits and court cards.

### The Major Arcana

**THE FOOL (0):** A new phase of life begins; the discovery of talents; new experiences; a risk must be take; there's a need to abandon the old and start something; personal growth; new development.

**THE MAGICIAN (1):** Possibilities in a person; new skills are available; potential is growing; opportunities and adventures unfolding; success in everything if a person utilizes his/her skills and talents.

## Chapter Nine: Advance Techniques Part III

**THE EMPRESS (2):** Known as the mother of fertility and growth; new things about to enter a situation; there may be a birth coming or a new path in life; focuses on marriage, relationship, pregnancy, patience and motherhood.

**THE EMPEROR (3):** A need to make something solid or to solidify something; focuses on building an idea or something with a firm structure; have values of authority, control and dominance; man of power; an employer or an authority.

**THE HIGH PRIESTESS (4):** A time for reflection; allows secrets to be revealed; shows potential abundance; urges people to pay attention to your dreams and intuition; this card is all about truly understanding life's possibilities.

**THE HIEROPHANT (5):** There's a need for spiritual purpose; talks about the search for a personal philosophy; encourages a person to increase studying and learning; focuses on humility and teachings; makes a person get through deeply frightening and hard situations; this card

## Chapter Nine: Advance Techniques Part III

can sometimes suggest marriage or a serious turn towards religion.

**THE LOVERS (6):** A love affair with a trial or choice attached; this card indicates that these decisions or choices are incredibly important and significant; one must choose the right path; a sign of true partnership; it focuses in choosing intuitively rather than by the use of intellect.

**THE CHARIOT (7):** Conflict within; struggles and battles; potential for victory; resolution of fights; moving forward; overcoming opposition through confidence; control and determination; it can also mean a journey or change of location.

**JUSTICE (8):** Need for clarity of mind; impartial judgment; requires a balanced intellect; legal matters needing attention; calls for the fairest decision; a person is also being called to account for one's actions and will be judged accordingly

## Chapter Nine: Advance Techniques Part III

**THE TEMPERANCE (9):** Harmony within relationships; suggests happy marriage or partnership; adaptation and coordination; balance; patience; moderation.

**THE STRENGTH (10):** Suggests a person must face the things or the truth in a situation that you have been putting off for too long; overcoming one's fears or doubts; courage; inner will; optimism.

**THE HERMIT (11):** A time for withdrawal; promotes silent meditation and solitude; patience is needed to confront one's inner world; could be someone who likes to or needs to work alone.

**THE WHEEL OF FORTUNE (12):** Change in fortune; new beginning; suggests new chapter in life; the Wheel makes a new turn; remain optimistic; someone who have faith that the Universe will take care of the situation.

## Chapter Nine: Advance Techniques Part III

**THE HANGED MAN (13):** Sacrifice must be made to gain something of greater value; talks about waiting in order to allow new possibilities to arise; vulnerability; selflessness; new perspectives; suggests a willingness to adapt in changing circumstances.

**DEATH (14):** Known as the most misunderstood card in the deck; the end of something which has been lived out; suggests transformation or new beginnings will follow; this card indicates a time of significant change and transition.

**THE DEVIL (15):** A confrontation with the inner world; facing fears and inhibitions can foster growth; the Devil reflects actual addictions and dependencies in one's life like alcohol, illegal drugs, toxic relationships, gambling, overspending; it also suggest breaking of bad or unhealthy habits or vices.

## Chapter Nine: Advance Techniques Part III

**THE TOWER (16):** Focuses on breaking down existing forms; changing false structures and finding true values; change around the home; emotionally challenging periods in a person's life; a time of great upheaval; it symbolizes conflict and overall disruption but it's for the greater good.

**THE STAR (17):** It's about facing things you have been reluctant to deal with; it could lead to good or bad things but this action needs to done.

**THE MOON (18):** Fluctuation; uncertainty; confusion; passive; suggests of letting go of one's conscious mental blocks; encourages a person to allow his/her intuition to guide him/her.

**THE SUN (19):** Optimism; passive; energetic or vitality; abundance time of clear vision; it is about embracing your destiny and giving it everything you have got; suggests happiness, triumph and good health; it also relates to

## Chapter Nine: Advance Techniques Part III

achievement; sometimes talks about traveling to a warm or tropical climate.

**JUDGEMENT (20):** It's a time for reaping rewards for past actions and reaching conclusions; suggests that a person may have assessed and evaluated his/her past experiences and have learned from them; rebirth or renewal; changes for the better; getting well after a long sickness; also suggests finding a new career or spiritual path.

**THE WORLD (21):** Success; achievement; attainment; the realization of a goal or the completion of a cycle; can also indicate world travel; suggests a feeling of being welcome anywhere you go.

### The Minor Arcana

**Wands Suit:** Wands is related to one's imagination and creativity, it is associated with the element of fire. It also focuses on action and movement and has risk – taking

# Chapter Nine: Advance Techniques Part III

qualities to it as well as confidence, inward passion and enthusiasm.

**Court Cards:**

## PAGE OF WANDS

- Serves as the instigator
- Curious and restless
- Suggests a creative Spark

## KNIGHT OF WANDS

- Adventurer
- Has a youthful enthusiasm
- Has appetite for risks
- Someone who is in search for challenge and excitement

## QUEEN OF WANDS

- Usually motivated and dynamic
- Someone who knows how to multi – task
- She's a heroine and charming but can also be selfish at times

## Chapter Nine: Advance Techniques Part III

**KING OF WANDS**

- Has a forceful personality
- Visionary
- Willful
- Reckless
- Extremely creative and inventive
- Sometimes it can also mean that he's not paying attention to details

**Pip Cards:**

**ACE OF WANDS (1)**

- Has a lot of creative energy, drive and vitality
- Has potential for success
- Initiative
- Boundless Energy
- Creative Power and Inspiration

**TWO OF WANDS**

- Suggests a more intuitive choice
- Two possibilities or duality
- Suggests equally good
- Firm plans should be done
- Envisioning the future

## Chapter Nine: Advance Techniques Part III

- Readiness for change
- Suggests that a person is standing in his past and future

**THREE OF WANDS**

- Suggests a stage of initial completion of a creative project
- Ideas are forming
- There are forces of new energy that is being generated
- Readiness to embark on a new adventure
- Taking opportunities
- Can also be about travelling

**FOUR OF WANDS**

- A time to pause for celebration after hard efforts
- Also suggests that a person should take a break, have a period of rest and learn to relax
- Sometimes it's known as the marriage card
- Harmony in one's home
- Aesthetic pleasures
- Positive connections

## Chapter Nine: Advance Techniques Part III

**FIVE OF WANDS**

- A time of struggle
- Challenges will constantly appear
- Expect difficulties ahead
- Open conflict
- Certain issues cause a lot of tension and confusion
- Lacking focus
- Suggests inner conflict or general chaos
- Can also mean that an individual is being pulled in different directions

**SIX OF WANDS**

- Public recognition
- Promotion
- Recognition for one's work
- Suggest success in any chosen field
- Supportive community

**SEVEN OF WANDS**

- Stiff competition must now be faced
- A person should holds one's ground
- Renewed determination
- Courage is necessary

## Chapter Nine: Advance Techniques Part III

- Suggests inner or outer battles
- It can also mean that an individual is prepared for a fight

**EIGHT OF WANDS**

- It's a card of ease, everything is happening in a fast pace
- There's a real sense of harmony
- Swiftness
- It's a period of fruitful progress after a delay or struggle
- Suggests that everything is in a person's favor but needs to continue pushing forward

**NINE OF WANDS**

- Strength in reserve can provide enough energy to win the battle
- The energy of a person seems exhausted but it suggests that one should still move forward to reach completion
- Requires perseverance
- Acknowledges weariness before a resolution can occur

# Chapter Nine: Advance Techniques Part III

## TEN OF WANDS

- There could be a danger implied in taking on more than one can cope with
- Inadequate awareness of one's limitations
- Can also mean that the passion can be renewed since a new cycle is coming
- It means a release from struggle

**Cups Suit:** The cups card is the suit that is related to the element of water. It relates to the inner realm not just pertaining to a person's emotions but also one's unconscious mind, dreams and intuition. It can also relate to relationships but in a deeper way.

**Court Cards:**

## PAGE OF CUPS

- Vulnerable
- Introspection
- Emotional Sensitivity

## Chapter Nine: Advance Techniques Part III

**KNIGHT OF CUPS**

- Dreamer
- Soft spoken
- Easy going and gentle
- Sincere

**QUEEN OF CUPS**

- Emotionally intense
- Can be intuitive and determined
- Can also be jealous and ruthless

**KING OF CUPS**

- Has a strong and controlling force
- Resists change in an emotional status quo
- One who likes to maintain power especially in relationships

**Pip Cards:**

**ACE OF CUPS (1)**

- High feelings and emotion
- New relationships
- Love affair

## Chapter Nine: Advance Techniques Part III

- The birth of a child
- Self – acceptance
- Spiritual guidance
- Gratitude and compassion

## TWO OF CUPS

- Commitment to romance
- Partnership or friendship
- Emotional balance
- There's an attraction of two things or people even if it comes from different natures

## THREE OF CUPS

- Suggest a celebration
- A time for rejoicing
- The commitment to a future project or endeavor has been made
- Suggests social life and successful partnerships/groups even from different natures
- Compatibility

## Chapter Nine: Advance Techniques Part III

**FOUR OF CUPS**

- Usually the person is self-absorbed
- An individual is content with the way things are
- Stability and confinement in terms of emotion
- There's an emotional uncertainty or self – doubt
- Someone who is not sure if they want to make a change
- Inability to make decisions
- Emotionally stuck

**FIVE OF CUPS**

- Regret over past actions
- Loss or betrayal in love
- Separation
- All is not lost even though it suggests loss
- Suggests that one should recognize what has been lost

**SIX OF CUPS**

- Past effort may bring present rewards
- Can also mean that an old lover may appear again
- Sentimental time
- Also known as a sibling card
- Mutual enjoyment in partnership

# Chapter Nine: Advance Techniques Part III

## SEVEN OF CUPS

- Focuses on several choice available
- Careful decisions must be made
- Action
- There is a risk of illusion
- You need to avoid escapism protect yourself against unclear thinking
- Also suggests search for wisdom or oneself
- Emotional confusion
- Self – doubt and can also be about projection of problems into the outer world and how one should take responsibility for it

## EIGHT OF CUPS

- Can mean that a person must leave the past behind
- Letting go of something even if it required much effort
- Suggests of walking away
- Encourages a person to pursue one's dream or ambitions
- Change of relationship status
- Emotional detachment
- Has willingness to walk into the unknown

Chapter Nine: Advance Techniques Part III

**NINE OF CUPS**

- A wish of paramount importance will come true
- Feelings of tremendous joy
- An emotional journey is almost over or will come to fruition
- Contentment

**TEN OF CUPS**

- Happiness and contentment
- A sense of permanence and future purpose
- It often suggests starting a family
- The sense of harmony
- Also suggests marriage
- Can also indicate responsibilities within a community

**Swords Suit:** deals with how people speak, how one perceives the world, an individual's belief system, how one makes decisions and understand things. The suit of Swords has the most problematic points in the tarot deck but it is the nature of air and the mind.

## Chapter Nine: Advance Techniques Part III

**Court Cards:**

### PAGE OF SWORDS

- Has a quality of wit and carelessness
- Also suggests immature thoughts

### KNIGHT OF SWORDS

- Communicator
- Someone who loves to learn and interested in new ideas
- Very expressive or talkative

### QUEEN OF SWORDS

- Advocate
- Someone who has high principles
- Doesn't compromise or negotiate
- Someone who is emotional and critical

### KING OF SWORDS

- Enforcer
- Someone who upholds the laws or values
- One who leads and decides
- Sometimes unsympathetic

# Chapter Nine: Advance Techniques Part III

**Pip Cards**

## ACE OF SWORDS (1)

- Inevitable and irrevocable change
- Awakening of mental powers
- Conflict can somehow arise at the start but are ultimately beneficial to the growth of the person
- Also called the sword of polarity or the sword of absolute knowledge
- It's a card of mind empowerment

## TWO OF SWORDS

- Stalemate; ambiguity
- Nothing can move or change
- Suggests great tension or deep hostility
- A person must make choices
- Having an inner focus in oneself
- Can also be about denial

## THREE OF SWORDS

- Quarrels and conflict
- A period of challenges or flux for relationships
- It also suggests that something sad or painful must be allowed to work something out

## Chapter Nine: Advance Techniques Part III

- Heartbreak or pain
- Disappointment; delusions
- Also suggest healing and assessment of situation

## FOUR OF SWORDS

- A need for rest or retreat after stress
- A time for reconciliation after tension
- Recuperation
- Suggests peace despite turmoil
- Postponement of decisions

## FIVE OF SWORDS

- Also known as the boundary card
- Indicates contradiction
- Pride must be swallowed
- Limitations must be recognized before further progress can be made
- Suggests that a person must work within the framework of that situation

## SIX OF SWORDS

- A card of harmony
- A period of calm after great anxiety

## Chapter Nine: Advance Techniques Part III

- Release of tension
- A peaceful journey towards smoother waters
- Also suggest that a person should physically move away from unpleasant environment
- Indicates physical travel or postponement of decision because the mind is inactive

### SEVEN OF SWORDS

- A need for evasion and avoidance of direct confrontation in order to achieve a goal
- One must be use his/her logical thinking, tact, and diplomacy instead of aggression
- Avoidance of conflict
- Sometimes known as the card of deceit or secrets
- Sometimes not wanting to face something or someone who hides the truth

### EIGHT OF SWORDS

- A fear of moving out of a situation in relationships
- Can also suggests a situation of tension but in this case, the choices are perfectly conscious
- It also talks about how one's perceptions block the will
- There could be fear of change

## Chapter Nine: Advance Techniques Part III

- The belief system could get a person stuck which is why the card suggests that an individual must think of something or perceive something in a different way

**NINE OF SWORDS**

- A time in which the mind is experiencing fears due to bad thought
- Nightmares and fantasies trouble the mind of the individual
- Can also mean that the end of mental struggle is near
- Anxiety and being overwhelmed
- There's a sense of worry and doom

**TEN OF SWORDS**

- The end of a painful situation or state
- There emerges an ability to see a situation practicality
- A fresh start is expected
- The start of the new cycle is about to begin which brings new hope
- A new horizon is near despite of the previous struggles

# Chapter Nine: Advance Techniques Part III

**Pentacles Suit:** the suit of pentacles is not just about money or financial matters; it's also about tangible or material things. It's also about the practical and pragmatic side, the stability and security in the physical world. It's also about how one's belief system, spirituality and creative tendencies play out in one's life.

**Court Cards:**

## PAGE OF PENTACLES

- Apprentice
- Someone who has a plan and undertakes a long term activity
- Indicates new beginnings and new perspective
- Someone who is earnest and grounded

## KNIGHT OF PENTACLES

- Worker
- Someone who is reliable and more mechanical
- Resourceful
- Doesn't move fast and takes his time in doing something

## Chapter Nine: Advance Techniques Part III

- Someone who exert steady effort to achieve something

## QUEEN OF PENTACLES

- Nurturer
- Represents constancy and comfort
- Someone who is self – employed and one who takes charge of their own life
- Calm but not complacent
- Industrious

## KING OF PENTACLES

- Entrepreneur
- Somebody who knows how to make money and provides security
- Someone who knows how to build things that will last

**Pip Cards:**

## ACE OF PENTACLES (1)

- Material achievement is possible

# Chapter Nine: Advance Techniques Part III

- Financial aid may be available for the beginning of a new venture
- New opportunities that is related to work or home
- New growth in every aspect of one's life (home, health, career)

## TWO OF PENTACLES

- Change and fluctuation in financial matters
- There'll be optimism and enthusiasm which balances out the anxieties when it comes to financial matters
- Transition
- There could be some sort of instability but not chaotic
- Flexible and can have many options, the key is to being open

## THREE OF PENTACLES

- A satisfactory period for a person
- Initial completion of work
- A basic structure is built which still requires further development
- Can indicate effective partnerships or collaboration
- Has a firm foundation

## Chapter Nine: Advance Techniques Part III

## FOUR OF PENTACLES

- There is danger in clinging too tightly to whatever a person has gained or accumulated
- Nothing is lost, but nothing can be gained either
- Resistance to change
- Focuses on self – preservation or maintaining one's position

## FIVE OF PENTACLES

- Financial loss and hardship
- Loss of luck especially in health
- Loss on a deeper level of self - confidence
- Loss of faith in oneself or life
- Expectation of failure
- Deprivation mentality
- Can indicate lack of spiritual connection

## SIX OF PENTACLES

- Help from a generous friend or employer
- Suggest a situation in which there is money or good fortune to be shared among people
- Shared resources
- Mutually beneficial

## Chapter Nine: Advance Techniques Part III

**SEVEN OF PENTACLES**

- A difficult decision must be made between material security and uncertain new opportunities
- Focuses about patience and taking time to make things happen
- There's availability of options
- Suggests reevaluation and can also indicate lack of motivation

**EIGHT OF PENTACLES**

- The apprentice, training or starting out a new endeavor in another profession
- Re- arrangement or re- alignment of priorities in any aspect
- One should take a new focus

**NINE OF PENTACLES**

- A card of great satisfaction and pleasure
- There'll be a reward for effort or material benefits
- Confidence in one's abilities
- Someone who celebrates life
- Appreciation for the good thing that is happening in one's life

# Chapter Nine: Advance Techniques Part III

- Someone who is self - reliant

## TEN OF PENTACLES

- Financial stability and foundation for home and family
- A new phase in life is about to come
- Denotes values of society, cultural traditions, morals and marriage (something that is unlikely to change or something that is secure).

# Chapter Nine: Advance Techniques Part III

## Chapter Ten: Conclusion

In this age when self – help books are increasingly becoming popular and reaching the top of the sales charts, it is quite apparent that more and more humans are no longer content to live our lives without direction. People usually search for the perfect techniques on which they can improve themselves upon. We now read self – help books, attend seminars, and also spend time perhaps every day in pursuit

## Chapter Ten: Conclusion

of our own quests. These kinds of measure can be effective for some people.

However for others they realize that something is missing; they have a goal but perhaps quite uncertain when it comes to deciding the best road to take. Unfortunately due to uncertainty, these people become depressed and sometimes do nothing to make their lives better.

As you've learned from this book, divination can provide us with essential information and also presents us with a view of the path in which we are heading. Through analyzing this information and be able to apply it in our present lives, we can go around unpleasant situations and also improve our life's quality. This, and the knowledge that one can re – create his/ her future life before it happens are one of the greatest lessons that divination has to offer. This ancient art can also assist us in making plans, make it easier to decide especially when faced with difficult choices, and also provide order into our lives and that of others.

Keep in mind that past, present and future are not separate. They simultaneously exist in this very moment

## Chapter Ten: Conclusion

simply because they are one. If you keep this fact in mind, you can fully utilize it to your advantage. Time is only an illusion we need to organize our daily lives but if only we recognize its flexibility then we can truly move within it and stretch it.

Divination is not just an art that can satisfy one's natural curiosity because the concepts presented can truly provide invaluable information. And using the responses that you receive will definitely help you build a more fulfilling and positive journey.

# Chapter Ten: Conclusion

# Index

active .................................................................................... 7, 77, 79, 86, 92

altar ................................................................................................................ 18

ancestors ............................................................................... 2, 5, 6, 35, 36, 50

ancient ................... 3, 4, 2, 3, 5, 13, 16, 17, 19, 20, 22, 23, 25, 29, 35, 51, 59, 93, 125, 137

ancient art ................................................ 2, 3, 5, 16, 17, 20, 23, 25, 125, 137

answer .......................................... 3, 10, 11, 14, 26, 32, 65, 66, 67, 69, 70, 137

art 1, 2, 5, 6, 9, 15, 16, 19, 23, 24, 26, 30, 32, 46, 71, 126

Babylonians ................................................................... 17, 18, 19, 28, 51

binary .................................................................... 10, 11, 12, 13, 26, 27, 43

Book of Changes ................. 3, 7, 58, 59, 60, 61, 62, 63, 64, 65, 66, 67, 68, 69, 70, 134, 135

cultures ................................................................................ 6, 7, 9, 37, 51, 93

deities ................................................................................... 6, 17, 18, 37, 51

destiny ............................................................................................ 4, 47, 50, 100

divination ........................................................................................... 4, 1, 2, 3,
  5, 6, 7, 8, 10, 12, 13, 15, 16, 17, 18, 19, 20, 21, 23, 24, 25, 26, 29, 30, 31, 32, 38, 41,
  42, 43, 45, 46, 47, 48, 49, 50, 51, 52, 53, 54, 55, 58, 93, 125, 134, 135, 136

divinatory ................................................................... 2, 9, 11, 13, 24, 30, 38, 40

diviner ............................................... 6, 10, 11, 12, 18, 20, 21, 24, 30, 32, 45, 46

effective ............................................................................ 3, 25, 30, 55, 120, 124

energies .................................................................................................. 6, 8, 33

experience ............................................................................. 24, 49, 65, 67, 94

fate .............................................................................................. 4, 7, 20, 47

forces ............................................................................. 3, 8, 13, 36, 37, 104

free will ........................................................................................................ 57

future ... 3, 2, 3, 4, 5, 6, 7, 8, 9, 10, 11, 12, 13, 14, 15, 17, 18, 22, 23, 25, 26, 27, 28, 31, 40, 41, 43, 45, 46, 47, 48, 49, 50, 51, 52, 53, 54, 55, 56, 57, 63, 74, 78, 103, 104, 109, 112, 125, 137

Germans .......................................................................................... 17, 20, 21

hieroglyphics ............................................................................................. 17

images .......................................................................... 11, 26, 32, 35, 62, 64, 70

improve ................................................................................... 4, 124, 125

interpretation ............................................... 2, 11, 12, 34, 35, 38, 39, 40, 54, 72, 75

intuition ................................................................................ 32, 63, 96, 100, 107

karma ................................................................................................ 52, 53

lives .............................................. 4, 3, 4, 5, 7, 14, 15, 26, 44, 48, 49, 52, 53, 124, 125, 126

manipulation ....................................................................................... 5, 9

methods .......................................................... 2, 18, 19, 24, 25, 28, 55, 134, 135

mind .. 3, 8, 12, 13, 32, 42, 49, 68, 69, 76, 87, 88, 94, 97, 107, 112, 114, 116, 117, 125, 134

mysterious ................................................................................. 15, 25, 52, 93

natural ................................................................................ 9, 31, 37, 45, 81, 126

observation .................................................................................. 5, 9, 11, 42

palms ............................................................................. 72, 73, 80, 83, 84

past . 1, 2, 3, 4, 6, 7, 13, 14, 23, 25, 45, 46, 47, 48, 49, 52, 64, 101, 104, 110, 111, 125, 137

path ..................................................................... 4, 38, 47, 48, 67, 96, 97, 101, 125

pictographs ....................................................................................... 35, 36, 37

positive ................................................................. 18, 27, 39, 51, 54, 55, 56, 67, 79, 126

practice ....................... 2, 3, 2, 6, 12, 16, 17, 19, 20, 21, 23, 24, 25, 26, 43, 45, 46, 47, 51 prediction ............................................................................................2, 9, 12, 26, 33

present ... 1, 2, 3, 4, 7, 8, 14, 16, 21, 23, 25, 38, 45, 46, 47, 48, 49, 53, 58, 63, 77, 110, 125, 137

process ..............................................................3, 7, 8, 10, 24, 25, 29, 30, 32, 48, 52, 53, 74, 76

psychic .................................................................................................3, 2, 12, 13, 134, 135

readings ..................................................................................................... 21, 26, 85, 134

relationship ...........................................................................................41, 42, 56, 96, 111

religious .............................................................................................................. 25, 37, 50

response ...................................................6, 8, 9, 11, 12, 27, 29, 31, 32, 41, 43, 51, 54, 55

rite ....................................................................................................................... 30, 32

rituals .................................................................................................... 5, 18, 31, 37, 51

Romans ..................................................................................................................... 17, 19

session ........................................................................................................................ 43

spiritual .................................................................... 6, 13, 25, 35, 63, 94, 96, 101, 121, 132

subject ........................................... 2, 18, 19, 62, 72, 75, 76, 77, 79, 80, 82, 85, 86, 88, 89, 90, 92

symbolism ............................................................................................... 35, 36, 37, 41, 64

symbols ............................................... 7, 11, 13, 26, 32, 34, 35, 36, 37, 38, 39, 40, 41, 43, 59

tarot deck ............................................................................................................... 94, 112

techniques 4, 1, 2, 3, 6, 8, 9, 10, 12, 13, 17, 18, 20, 23, 25, 26, 28, 31, 39, 43, 54, 124, 137

theory ............................................................................................................ 46, 47, 62, 63

thoughts ........................................................................................................ 3, 8, 40, 43, 113

Tibetans ...................................................................................................................... 17

Time .................................................................................................. 7, 44, 45, 47, 48, 74, 125

tool ......................................................................................................... 4, 45, 74, 135

universal forces ............................................................................................................. 3

warnings ................................................................................................. 7, 54, 55

# PHOTO REFERENCES

Page 1 Photo by user Glegle via Pixabay.com

https://pixabay.com/en/sky-divine-aurora-light-spiritual-437690/

Page 5 Photo by user spirit111 via Pixabay.com

https://pixabay.com/en/galaxy-fog-kosmus-universe-2357504/

Page 16 Photo by user kalhh via Pixabay.com

https://pixabay.com/en/creation-god-finger-clouds-light-1906289/

Page 23 Photo by user spirit111 via Pixabay.com

https://pixabay.com/en/cassiopeia-supernova-cassiopeia-2515913/

Page 34 Photo by user Waldo93 via Pixabay.com

https://pixabay.com/en/light-through-clouds-light-sunlight-1264548/

Page 44 Photo by user annca via Pixabay.com

https://pixabay.com/en/pocket-watch-time-of-sand-time-3156771/

Page 50 Photo by user geralt via Pixabay.com

https://pixabay.com/en/sky-clouds-clouds-form-3335585/

Page 58 Photo by user spirit111 via Pixabay.com

https://pixabay.com/en/galaxy-fog-kosmus-universe-2357502/

Page 71 Photo by user SookyungAn via Pixabay.com

https://pixabay.com/en/the-palm-of-your-hand-hand-palmistry-2704020/

Page 93 Photo by user aubryal via Pixabay.com

https://pixabay.com/en/clairvoyance-map-tarot-2951517/

Page 124 Photo by user Lars_Nissen_Photoart via Pixabay.com

https://pixabay.com/en/winter-light-shadow-snow-2080327/

# REFERENCES

**Methods of Divination** – Thoughtco.com
https://www.thoughtco.com/methods-of-divination-2561764

**An Introduction to Using Divination Tools** – Wicca.com
https://wicca.com/celtic/divination/intro.htm

**Divination: We All Just Want to Know What's Coming Next** – PsychologyToday.com
https://www.psychologytoday.com/intl/blog/myth-the-mind/201801/divination-we-all-just-want-know-what-s-coming-next

**Divination for Beginners Reading the Past, Present & Future** – Llewelly.com
https://www.llewellyn.com/product_excerpt.php?ean=9780738703848&excerpt_id=3072

**Methods of Divination** - Psychic-readings-guide.com
https://www.psychic-readings-guide.com/methods-of-divination/

**Book of Changes – The Book of Changes** - Divination.com
https://divination.com/iching/

**Which divination method is right for you? Five ways to explore psychic gifts** - Groveandgrotto.com
https://www.groveandgrotto.com/blogs/articles/which-divination-method-is-right-for-you-five-ways-to-explore-psychic-gifts

**A Beginner's Guide to Tarot** - Beliefnet.com
https://www.beliefnet.com/inspiration/a-beginners-guide-to-tarot.aspx

**How Does Divination with Tarot Work?** – Keen.com
https://www.keen.com/articles/tarot/how-does-divination-with-tarot-work

**Past, Present & Future** – MyDivination.com
http://www.mydivination.com/ViewCategory.mdv?Category=PastPresFuture

**Methods of Divination** – Palmistry - Psychiclight.com
https://www.psychiclight.com/methods-of-divination-palmistry/

**The Basics of Book of Changes, the Chinese Divination Tool** - Fractalenlightenment.com
https://fractalenlightenment.com/14154/spirituality/the-basics-of-i-ching-the-chinese-divination-tool

**4 Divination Tools and How to Use Them** - Tesswhitehurst.com
https://tesswhitehurst.com/4-divination-tools-how-to-use-them/

**Divination Tools** – Thoughtco.com
https://www.thoughtco.com/divination-tools-4053396

**The 10 Most Common Types of Divination Tools Used By Psychics** - Psychicgurus.org
https://www.psychicgurus.org/divination-tools/

**Divination Tools** - Paganspath.com
https://www.paganspath.com/meta/divinationtools.htm

www.ingramcontent.com/pod-product-compliance
Lightning Source LLC
LaVergne TN
LVHW051838080426
835512LV00018B/2938